Foreword

Chapter 1

Introduction

Welcome to The Evolution of Keeping Time, a journey not just through the annals of history to uncover the roots and routes of timekeeping, but a voyage into understanding how this quest shapes our present and can mold our future. Inspired by the pragmatic and adventurous approach of Tim Ferris, this book is crafted for the curious minds of young adults, eager to hack the code of productivity and personal growth by gleaning wisdom from the past.

In our fast-paced digital age, time feels more like a commodity than ever before. We're inundated with tools, apps, and methods promising to help us manage our time better, to become more productive, to squeeze more out of each day. But to truly master the art of time management, perhaps we need to look back before we can leap forward. That's what this book intends to do.

Through the lens of timekeeping's evolution, we'll explore how humanity's endeavor to measure and manage time reflects deeper truths about our values, priorities, and the relentless human spirit of innovation. From the shadows cast by the first sundials to the atomic precision of today's clocks, each chapter unveils not just a history lesson but a mirror reflecting our perennial struggle and triumph over the intangible force of time.

But this isn't just a history book. Infused with the spirit of Tim Ferris's teachings, The Evolution of Keeping Time is about applying the lessons of the past to the challenges of the present. It's about understanding that the devices we've created to segment, manage, and measure time are more than inventions; they're reflections of human ingenuity, culture, and the incessant quest for efficiency and growth.

As we delve into the past, with pencil-drawn illustrations bringing each timekeeping device to life, we'll draw parallels to today's quest for productivity and personal development. You'll see how the evolution of timekeeping devices mirrors our own journey towards self-improvement and mastery over our most precious resource: time.

So, whether you're looking to enhance your productivity, understand the deeper philosophical implications of time, or simply indulge in the fascinating history of human innovation, this book offers a unique perspective. It's a reminder that understanding the past can illuminate the path to a more intentional, efficient, and fulfilling life.

Let's embark on this temporal odyssey together, unraveling the fabric of timekeeping to weave the tapestry of our own time well spent. Welcome to The Time of Your Life.

Chapter 2

The Dawn of Timekeeping

Observing the Cosmos

As humanity gazed upward, the vast expanse of the cosmos offered not just beauty and wonder but also a means to measure the passage of time. This chapter retraces the steps of ancient civilizations as they embarked on the earliest attempts to understand and keep time through the regular movements of celestial bodies. It explores the genesis of timekeeping through celestial clockwork and the monumental efforts to align human life with the cosmos.

Celestial Clockwork:

The Cosmos as a Timekeeper

Long before the invention of clocks and calendars, ancient peoples turned their eyes skyward to divine the time. They observed the regular patterns of the sun, moon, and stars, recognizing these celestial movements as reliable markers of time. This section delves into how different civilizations harnessed these observations to create the world's first calendars, marking not just days but also significant seasonal and agricultural events. From the lunar cycles that demarcated months to the sun's path dictating the solstices and equinoxes, early humans found in the heavens a clock of incomparable precision and reliability.

The reliance on celestial bodies was not merely practical. It also bore deep spiritual significance, with many cultures believing the heavens to be the realm of gods and the timing of celestial events to be divine messages. Thus, the act of timekeeping became an intertwined practice of observation, religion, and societal regulation, guiding everything from farming to festivals.

The desire to comprehend and celebrate the celestial order led to the creation of monumental structures that stand as testament to humanity's ingenuity and reverence for the cosmos. This section examines megalithic structures, such as Stonehenge, and their roles in early astronomical observations and ceremonial timekeeping.

Stonehenge, perhaps the most iconic of these ancient observatories, was meticulously aligned with the summer solstice sunrise, serving as a giant calendar made of stone. Similar structures around the world, from the Karnak (a temple plaza in Egypt) to the Sun Dagger in the American Southwest, reveal a global pattern of constructing megaliths for marking celestial events. These structures were not only feats of engineering and astronomy but also sacred sites that connected the earthly realm with the celestial, hosting gatherings that celebrated the cyclical nature of time.

Through detailed pencil-drawn illustrations, we visualize ancient peoples congregated around these monumental stones, their faces lifted in awe and reverence towards the sky. The drawings capture the essence of these gatherings, highlighting the significance of such monuments in early astronomical observation and ceremonial timekeeping. The illustrations depict these ancient practices with a sense of wonder, showcasing the deep connection our ancestors felt with the cosmos and their relentless pursuit to synchronize human existence with the celestial cycles.

In marrying observation with spiritual significance, these early efforts at timekeeping laid the foundational understanding of the cosmos as a clockwork of celestial bodies. They remind us of our perpetual fascination with the heavens and our enduring quest to measure our place within the vast tapestry of the universe.

Chapter 3

Water Clocks

Water Flows Time Shows

As civilizations evolved, so did their methods for measuring time. Emerging from the shadow of sundials, water clocks, or clepsydras, (ancient time keeping device) marked a significant advancement in timekeeping technology. These devices, which measured time through the flow of water, were among the first attempts to quantify time independently of the celestial bodies.

This chapter explores the invention and spread of water clocks across cultures, delving into their mechanics, their varied uses in society, and their everlasting legacy.

Water clocks appeared in various forms across ancient civilizations, from Babylon and Egypt to Greece and China, each adapting the technology to their specific needs and understanding of the world. The basic principle behind a water clock is simple: time is measured by the amount of water that flows from one container to another. However, within this simplicity lay the potential for remarkable innovation.

The mechanics of water clocks evolved significantly over time. The Greeks, for example, used a straightforward method where water dripped at a constant rate from one vessel to another, with marks on the interior indicating the passing hours. In contrast, the Chinese developed more complex water clocks with gears and flow regulators, enabling more accurate and consistent time measurement. Meanwhile, Islamic inventors created water clocks of extraordinary complexity, featuring automata (a machine that operates on it's own) that performed at specific times, turning timekeeping into a spectacle of engineering and art.

Water clocks were more than just timekeeping devices; they played crucial roles in governance, religion, and daily life across different societies. In ancient Egypt, water clocks were used to allocate irrigation water, a critical resource for agriculture. In Greece, they regulated speakers' time in public debates, ensuring fairness and order. The Islamic world saw them as marvels of engineering that demonstrated the harmony between scientific knowledge and spiritual beliefs.

To gain deeper insight into the legacy of water clocks, an interview with a historian specializing in ancient timekeeping technologies reveals the profound impact these devices had on society. They highlight how water clocks enabled societies to organize time in ways that were previously impossible, facilitating the administration of cities, the observance of religious practices, and the structuring of daily life around a more precise understanding of time.

The story of water clocks teaches us the importance of flow and consistency in time management. Just as the steady drip of water marked the passage of hours, so too must we learn to pace ourselves in our endeavors. The water clock serves as a metaphor for life, reminding us that a constant, steady flow of effort can lead to remarkable achievements over time.

As we reflect on the legacy of water clocks, we're reminded of humanity's enduring quest to measure and manage time. These ancient devices, captured in the pencil-drawn illustrations of this chapter, represent a pivotal chapter in the history of timekeeping, showcasing the ingenuity and creativity of our ancestors. Through the steady flow of water, they found a way to bring order to their world, laying the groundwork for the future of timekeeping.

Chapter 4

The Tic of History

Clockwork and the Industrial Age

The Middle Ages witnessed a revolution in timekeeping that would forever change humanity's relationship with time: the advent of mechanical clocks. This innovation marked a departure from natural and simpler mechanical methods to more sophisticated mechanisms, heralding a new era of precision and reliability in time measurement. The journey of mechanical clocks from their inception to becoming a cornerstone of societal organization is a tale of technical ingenuity, societal transformation, and the enduring human quest for accuracy and control over time.

The revolution began in the late 13th century, with the first mechanical clocks appearing in the towers of cathedrals and public buildings across Europe. Unlike their predecessors, these clocks did not rely on water flow or sundials but on a complex system of gears, weights, and escapements. The technical breakthroughs that made mechanical clocks possible—such as the verge-and-foliot (a device that permits controlled motion) escapement and later the more accurate pendulum—were monumental. They allowed for the measurement of time in equal segments, a concept that was revolutionary and laid the groundwork for the standardized timekeeping we take for granted today.

The impact of mechanical clocks on medieval society was profound. Installed in public squares and cathedrals, these clocks became symbols of communal life and order, regulating market times, religious services, and daily routines. The sound of bells ringing the hours became a shared experience, binding communities together in a collective awareness of time. Furthermore, mechanical clocks were instrumental in the navigation advancements of the Age of Exploration. Mariners could now more accurately measure time at sea, a critical factor in determining longitude and safely navigating the world's oceans.

Behind every clock tower and every mechanical timepiece were the clockmakers, artisans whose skill and dedication brought the gears of progress to life. Personal stories of notable clockmakers, such as Peter Henlein, who is credited with inventing the first portable timepiece, and Christiaan Huygens, who introduced the pendulum clock, highlight the blend of artistry and science that characterized this era. These individuals were not just technicians but visionaries who pushed the boundaries of what was mechanically possible, contributing to the advancement of timekeeping technology and, by extension, society itself.

The actionable takeaway from the story of mechanical clocks is the value of precision and the power of incremental improvement. Just as the evolution from the sundial to the mechanical clock was marked by gradual refinements and innovations, so too can small, precise advancements in our own lives lead to significant progress. The mechanical clock revolution teaches us that attention to detail and a commitment to improving upon the status quo can yield transformative results, both in technology and in personal growth.

Accompanying this chapter are pencil-drawn illustrations that vividly bring to life the mechanical clock revolution. From the grandeur of public clock towers to the intricate workings of gears and escapements and the focused dedication of the clockmakers, these illustrations capture the essence of an era that forever changed how we perceive and organize time. Through these visuals, we not only gain a deeper appreciation for the craftsmanship and inovation of the Middle Ages but are also reminded of the enduring human endeavor to measure, manage, and master time.

Chapter 5

Pocket watches

Portable Time

The evolution of timekeeping from the public spectacle of clock towers to the intimate realm of the pocket watch marked a significant turn in the history of time. This transition not only reflected technological advancements but also a profound change in the perception of time as a personal commodity. The journey of pocket watches from their inception in the 16th century to becoming indispensable accessories in the 19th century encapsulates a period of intense innovation and societal transformation.

The craftsmanship and innovation behind the first pocket watches were remarkable. Born out of the necessity for portability, these timepieces were engineering marvels of their age. Early pocket watches were bulky and primarily worn around the neck or carried in a purse. However, as watchmaking skills advanced, they became more compact and intricate, featuring ornate designs that reflected the status and taste of their owners. The inner workings of these watches, with their gears, springs, and escapement mechanisms, were a testament to the watchmakers' skill and ingenuity.

Pocket watches soon transcended their practical purpose to become symbols of status and sophistication. Owning a finely crafted pocket watch was a sign of wealth and distinction. These timepieces were not just tools for telling time; they were fashion statements and personal treasures that reflected the owner's identity. The ritual of pulling out a pocket watch to check the time became a gesture of elegance and poise, influencing social behaviors and etiquette.

To delve deeper into the cultural significance of pocket watches, an interview with a collector or historian reveals the nuanced role these timepieces played in society. They highlight how pocket watches were integral to social interactions, with the presentation of one's watch serving as a subtle display of social standing. Furthermore, the interview explores how the pocket watch became a cherished heirloom, passed down through generations as a symbol of familial legacy and continuity.

The story of pocket watches teaches us the power of personal responsibility for time. As timekeeping became a personal affair, individuals were more conscious of their time management, marking a shift towards self-discipline and punctuality. The pocket watch served as a constant reminder of the value of time, encouraging its owner to use it wisely.

Accompanying this narrative are pencil-drawn illustrations that vividly capture the evolution and cultural significance of pocket watches. From the ornate designs of the 16th century to the detailed inner mechanisms and the portrayal of a gentleman with his timepiece, these illustrations highlight the technological marvels and cultural symbols that pocket watches became. Through these visuals, we gain a deeper appreciation for the artistry and societal impact of pocket watches, serving as a reminder of the era when time became a personal asset to be cherished and managed with care.

The journey from public clocks to the intimacy of the pocket watch not only reflects the progress of timekeeping technology but also the evolving relationship between individuals and time. In the ticking of these portable timepieces, we find a legacy of precision, personal responsibility, and the enduring human desire to capture and manage the fleeting moments of life.

Chapter 6

Quartz Watch

The Crystal Revolution

The advent of quartz technology in watchmaking marked a seismic shift in the industry, ushering in an era of unprecedented accuracy and reliability in timekeeping. This chapter explores the discovery of quartz crystal's piezoelectric (an electric charge that accumulates in quartz) properties, the development and impact of the first quartz watches, and the subsequent quartz crisis that reshaped the landscape of traditional watchmaking. Through personal insights from the engineers and designers who pioneered this technology, we uncover the challenges and triumphs of the quartz revolution and the lasting implications for innovation in timekeeping.

The story begins in the early 20th century with the discovery of the piezoelectric properties of quartz crystals. Scientists found that when a quartz crystal is subjected to an electrical charge, it vibrates at a highly stable and precise frequency. This property made quartz ideal for use in timekeeping, as the consistent vibrations could be converted into electronic pulses to measure time with remarkable accuracy. The first quartz clock was developed in the 1920s, but it was not until the 1960s that the technology was miniaturized enough to be used in wristwatches.

The launch of the first commercial quartz wristwatch in 1969 represented a technological breakthrough and a cultural phenomenon. These early quartz watches were not only more accurate than their mechanical counterparts but also more affordable, making precise timekeeping accessible to a broader audience.

The introduction of quartz technology into the watchmaking industry sparked a period of rapid innovation, leading to the development of features such as digital displays, alarm functions, and stopwatch capabilities, further solidifying the appeal of quartz watches.

However, the rise of quartz technology also precipitated the quartz crisis, a period of economic turmoil for traditional watchmakers. The accuracy, reliability, and lower cost of quartz watches posed a significant challenge to the mechanical watch industry, leading to a decline in demand for traditional timepieces and causing many storied brands to face financial difficulties or cease operations altogether. This crisis prompted a period of introspection and innovation within the industry, leading to a resurgence of interest in mechanical watchmaking as a craft and art form, alongside the continued popularity of quartz watches.

Personal insights from the engineers and designers who worked on the development of quartz watches highlight the spirit of experimentation and the challenges of pioneering a new technology. These individuals navigated uncharted territory, balancing the technical demands of quartz timekeeping with the aesthetic and functional expectations of watch wearers. Their stories underscore the importance of embracing change and innovation, even in the face of uncertainty and resistance.

The actionable takeaway from the quartz watch revolution is the power of embracing change and innovation. Just as the advent of quartz technology transformed the watchmaking industry, so too must we remain open to new ideas and approaches in our own lives and work. The story of quartz watches teaches us that innovation can lead to unprecedented advancements and opportunities, but it also requires the courage to venture into the unknown and the resilience to adapt to new challenges.

Accompanying this narrative are pencil-drawn illustrations that capture the pivotal moments of the quartz revolution, from the scientific discovery of quartz's properties to the excitement of the first commercial quartz watch and the contemplative figure of a traditional watchmaker facing a changing industry. These illustrations not only enhance our understanding of the technological and cultural impact of quartz watches but also serve as a visual testament to the enduring importance of innovation in the journey of progress.

Chapter 7

Digital Watches and Atomic Clocks

The transition from mechanical gears to digital displays and the advent of atomic clocks how digital watches revolutionized personal timekeeping and delves into the world of atomic represent monumental leaps in the quest for precision in timekeeping. This chapter explores clocks, which have redefined the very concept of time with unparalleled accuracy. Through interviews with scientists involved in atomic timekeeping, we gain insights into the technical challenges and breakthroughs that have marked this journey. The overarching theme is the relentless human pursuit of perfection and accuracy in measuring time.

Digital watches, emerging prominently in the 1970s, marked a significant departure from traditional mechanical watches. They introduced a new era where time could be displayed in digits on an LCD screen, a concept that was revolutionary. The appeal of digital watches lay not only in their novelty but in their added functionalities such as stopwatches, alarms, and later, smart capabilities that integrated seamlessly with daily life. The leap from mechanical to digital was more than a technological evolution; it signified a change in how people interacted with and perceived time—making it more accessible and manipulable than ever before.

Parallel to the rise of digital watches was the development of atomic clocks, which have set a new standard for accuracy in timekeeping. Atomic clocks do not rely on mechanical movements or electronic oscillations but on the properties of atoms, specifically the consistent vibration of cesium atoms. This method of timekeeping is so precise that the margin of error in an atomic clock is just one second in millions of years. The introduction of atomic clocks has had profound implications, not just for scientific research but for global telecommunications, navigation systems, and the synchronization of financial markets.

Developing atomic clocks presented numerous technical challenges, from isolating atoms to accurately measuring their vibrations. Interviews with scientists involved in atomic timekeeping shed light on the complexity of this endeavor. These experts discuss the initial skepticism, the experimental breakthroughs, and the collaborative efforts across disciplines that were necessary to make atomic clocks a reality. Their stories highlight the dedication and ingenuity required to push the boundaries of what is possible in time measurement.

The actionable takeaway from the evolution of digital watches and the development of atomic clocks is the importance of embracing change and pursuing accuracy. In the quest for perfection in timekeeping, each technological advancement has built on the past, demonstrating a continuum of innovation. The journey from mechanical to digital and atomic timekeeping underscores the value of precision and the impact that relentless improvement can have on technology and society.

Accompanying this narrative are pencil-drawn illustrations that vividly capture the milestones of this journey. From the sleek design of a digital watch to the intricate workings of an atomic clock and the collaborative spirit of scientists tackling complex challenges, these illustrations bring to life the themes of technological evolution and the pursuit of precision. Through these visuals, we are reminded of the collective endeavor to define and measure time, a quest that has led to the ultimate in accuracy and has forever altered our relationship with the seconds, minutes, and hours that shape our lives.

Chapter 8

Welcome in the Age of Silicon

The advent of smartwatches marks a significant milestone in the evolution of timekeeping, blending traditional watch functions with the capabilities of modern technology. This chapter explores how smartwatches have revolutionized our interaction with time, integrating features such as health tracking, notifications, and productivity tools into our daily lives. It delves into the potential future advancements in timekeeping technology and shares personal stories from the innovators and users at the forefront of this transformation. Through these narratives, we uncover the challenges and opportunities presented by the integration of timekeeping and technology, offering insights into how we can balance technological advancement with a personal connection to time.

Smartwatches have redefined our relationship with time by making it more interactive and personalized. Gone are the days when watches merely told time; today's smartwatches serve as fitness coaches, communication hubs, and personal assistants. They track our health metrics, remind us of important tasks, and even allow us to control smart home devices, all from our wrists. This multifunctionality has made smartwatches an indispensable part of many people's lives, enhancing our ability to manage time effectively and stay connected with what matters most.

Looking ahead, the future of timekeeping technology holds exciting possibilities. Innovations such as holographic displays, augmented reality interfaces, and even direct neural connections could further enhance the functionality of smartwatches, making them more intuitive and integrated into our daily routines. These advancements promise to transform our interaction with time, offering new ways to access information, communicate, and navigate the world around us.

Personal stories from the innovators behind smartwatch technology and the users who have integrated these devices into their lives highlight the impact of this technology on personal productivity, health, and well-being. From engineers who design the latest features to individuals who have found new motivation for fitness or better work-life balance through their devices, these narratives underscore the profound influence of smartwatches on our lives.

The actionable takeaway from the rise of smartwatches and the potential future of timekeeping is the importance of balancing technology and personal connection to time. As we embrace the convenience and capabilities of smartwatches, we must also remain mindful of the value of disconnecting, appreciating the moment, and fostering human connections that technology cannot replicate. The challenge lies in leveraging these devices to enhance our lives without letting them dictate our time or detract from the richness of unmediated experiences.

Accompanying this exploration are pencil-drawn illustrations that vividly depict the integration of smartwatches into daily life and imagine the future of timekeeping technology. From the practical applications of current devices to the conceptual designs of future innovations, these drawings capture the essence of smartwatches as both technological marvels and tools for personal empowerment. Through these visuals, we gain a deeper appreciation for the role of smartwatches in the

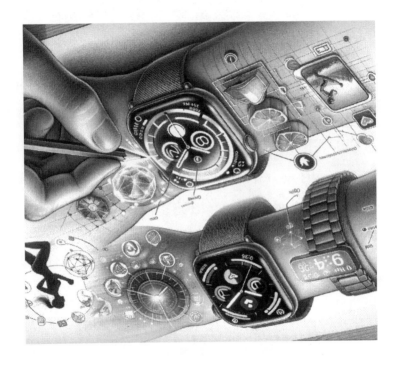

ongoing evolution of timekeeping, highlighting the balance between embracing technology and maintaining a meaningful connection to the time that shapes our lives.